GRANDMA'S GARDENS

written by

HILLARY CLINTON AND CHELSEA CLINTON

illustrated by

CARME LEMNISCATES

PHILOMEL BOOKS

Grandma Dorothy loved gardens. She loved the flowers. She loved the trees. She loved the animals that lived in the dirt and between the plants. And she loved the time she spent there with us. Because of Grandma Dorothy, we love gardens, too.

I remember dancing across the lawn
with sparklers in each hand.

I remember cutting up the tomatoes we'd just picked for our Fourth of July lunch.

Gardens are places for celebration.

I remember being so
proud that Grandma
asked me to help her care
for the azaleas.

I don't know whether Chelsea or my mom loved gardening together more.

Gardens help teach responsibility.

When my grandma talked about the gardens she visited in Morocco, she made me want to visit them, too.

I loved that my mom had adventures later in life—and that her adventures included beautiful gardens.

Gardens are places of discovery.

I loved reading with my grandmother
on her porch, next to her sunflowers, while
listening to the animals in the nearby zoo.

They often would read the same
book for their book club of two—or
three when we all read together.

Gardens are places for learning.

In Arkansas and Washington, D.C., we spent lots of time at the zoo, and my grandmother always pointed out the trees and plants the animals were sitting under, swinging on or eating.

I always appreciated my mom teaching Chelsea how dependent her favorite animals were on nature, whether they were caterpillars in the backyard or pandas at the zoo.

Gardens are homes to creatures large and small.

I loved listening to my mom and grandma talk about all the places in the world where our food comes from— including our own backyard.

As a little girl, I remember my mom explaining that some of my favorite foods, like peaches, were so special because they grew only during summer months.

Gardens give us food.

When my grandma moved in with my parents, I loved visiting them and listening to my mom and grandma talk about the newest additions to their garden.

Once we were living together, my mom and I spent even more time planning our garden, picking out and tending to the plants, trees and flowers, and watching the birds.

Gardens are where we can create beauty.

When I saw my grandma, I loved showing her pictures of the gardens I'd visited. When I could, I would bring souvenir books of the gardens to share; my grandma's smile made the heavy suitcase worth it.

As I traveled around the world, I always tried to store up the images of the gardens, plants and trees I'd seen to share with my mom. I loved sharing my memories with her.

Gardens are places to share stories.

My grandma gardened into her nineties. She knew it was good for her, but that's not why she did it. She did it because she loved it.

Watching my mom enjoying our garden and tending to it gave me as much joy as it gave her.

Gardens help us stay strong.

On a particularly magical day, my grandma and I visited
Mount Vernon, George Washington's home and gardens. I
wish we could have visited more gardens together.

My mom and I would go to historic Dumbarton Oaks near our home in Washington, D.C., to wander around the gardens and learn more about the family who had lived there. I wish we could have visited more gardens together.

Gardens are places to create memories.

My children now garden with their grandmother,
and I know Grandma Dorothy is present every time
we plant a vegetable or water a flower.

I feel particularly close to my mom when explaining
how to use a small shovel, how deep to plant a seed,
how much water a plant truly needs.

Gardens connect us across generations.

My grandmother was always willing to play tag with me, throw a ball around, play hide-and-seek in the garden. I think she had as much fun as I did.

Today, watching my grandchildren race across the lawn, run around the trees and smell the flowers makes my heart smile.

Gardens are places to remember.

Our beloved Grandma Dorothy believed in gratitude, in being thankful for what we've been given and working to expand our circle of blessings. We are so grateful she shared her love of gardens with us and we can share the love she gave us with the next generation.

What do you share with the people you love?

PHILOMEL BOOKS
An imprint of Penguin Random House LLC, New York

First published in the United States of America by Philomel Books,
an imprint of Penguin Random House LLC, 2020

Visit us online at penguinrandomhouse.com

Library of Congress Cataloging-in-Publication Data is available.
Manufactured in China by RR Donnelley Asia Printing Solutions Ltd.
ISBN 9780593115350

3 5 7 9 10 8 6 4 2

Edited by Jill Santopolo. Design by Ellice M. Lee.
Text set in Granjon. The illustrations were done in mixed media.

To grandmothers, grandchildren and gardeners everywhere.
—H.R.C. and C.C.